HOW AM...
TO LOVE SCHOOL AGAIN
A STORY ABOUT ADHD

HOW AMARi LEARNED TO LOVE SCHOOL AGAiN

A STORY ABOUT ADHD

SIGHT WORDS

EXCITED THRILLED DISAPPOINTED

OVERJOYED

Email us at
info@ghpsychiatry.com
ISBN-13: 978-0-9972605-6-4
ISBN-10: 0-9972605-6-4
TgosketchPress
Chicago, Illinois
www.tgosketch.com

Dedication:

We dedicate this book to our family, friends, and mentors that have tirelessly supported us on our journey.

We also dedicate this to all children and families, all of whom deserve to have a voice.

It was the first day of first grade, and Amari was so excited! He had fun in kindergarten and was thrilled to start school again.

"Hi, my name is Amari, and I'm a superhero. **MATH IS MY SUPERPOWER!**"

After a while, things started to change. Amari was having trouble staying focused and getting his work done in time.

Kindergarten had been so easy, and first grade seemed so hard...

Every little thing was grabbing his attention, and his friends could tell.

During recess, Amari and his friends played baseball. The ball was thrown right to Amari.

"SHHHHHH!"

"Sssshhhh!" Said the lady at church,
but Amari couldn't sit still, or stay quiet.

Amari's grades were falling.

"MATH IS MY SUPERPOWER."

He said to himself "How did I fail?" Amari was very disappointed.

Amari's teachers tried to help him in class, but he had a big case of the wiggles and could not pay attention.

Nothing seemed to help, and Amari felt like crying.

One day Amari's teacher called his parents and told them about his troubles in school.

His parents noticed Amari had problems at home also, like not listening, not following directions, not completing his chores and talking over other people.

His father said "There's nothing wrong with him, he will grow out of it. He acts just like I did when I was his age."

His mother felt differently saying "I think we should take Amari to be seen."

That night Amari's parents told him they would take him to get help, and that they loved him no matter what.

The next day at the doctor's office,
Amari's parents went over his problems. The
doctor started working to make things better.

The work Amari, his parents, the school and the doctor were doing helped him with paying attention in school and at home.

Amari moved to the front of the class where there were fewer distractions and he could see the teacher better.

At the end of the day, Amari's teacher would make sure he wrote down his homework correctly and would tell him all of the good things he did throughout the day.

Amari's parents put together a chore chart to help him organize.

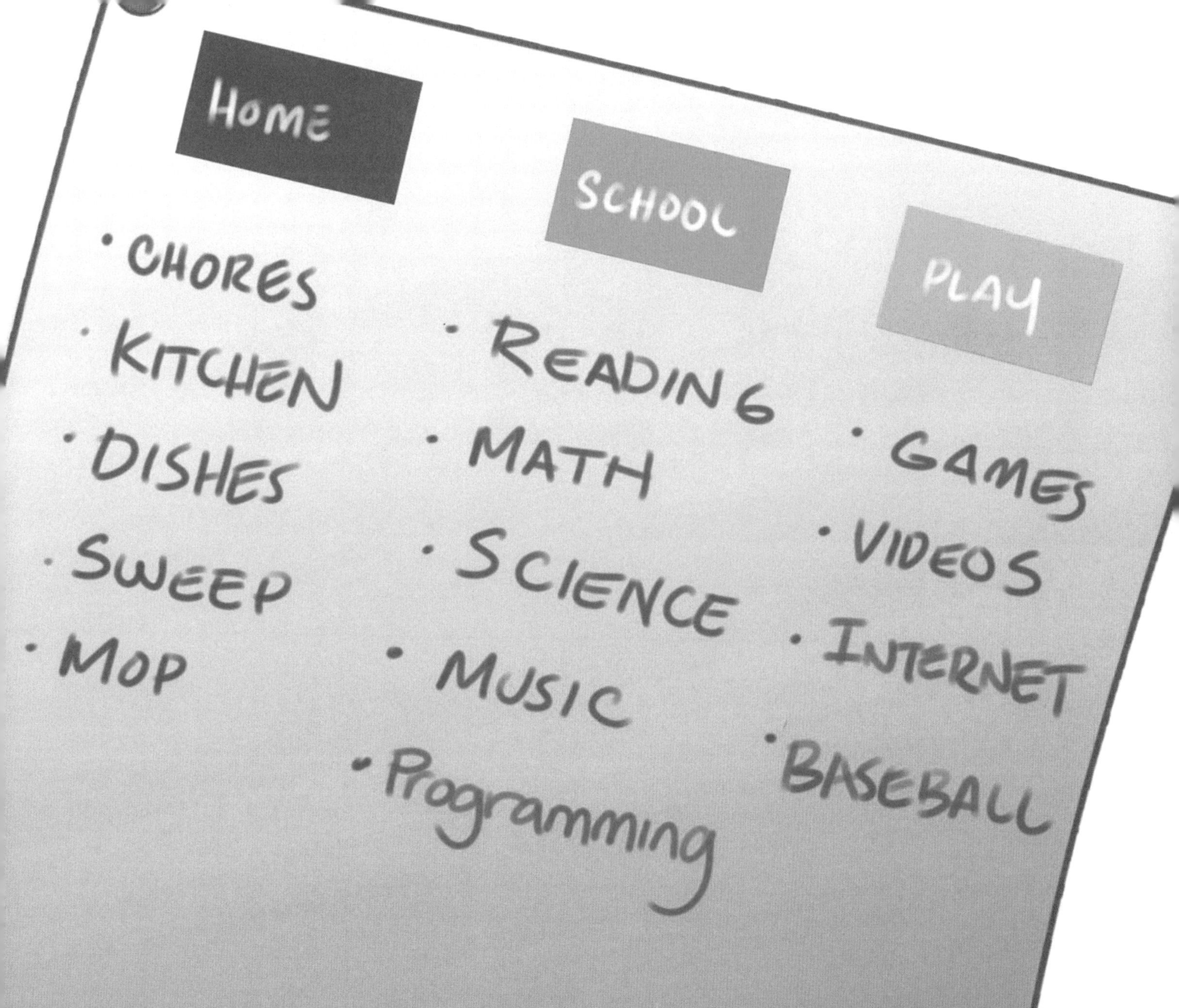

HOME

- CHORES
- KITCHEN
- DISHES
- SWEEP
- MOP

SCHOOL

- READING
- MATH
- SCIENCE
- MUSIC
- Programming

PLAY

- GAMES
- VIDEOS
- INTERNET
- BASEBALL

They also started giving him one task at a time. This helped Amari stay focused at home as well.

After just a few months Amari was pleased with school just as much as he was on his first day. He was back at the top of his class and having a ton of fun! His star was back and brighter than ever.

In no time Amari was a much better student.

"MY SUPERPOWERS ARE BACK!"

His parents noticed the difference as well. He finished his chores and followed directions with ease.

Amari's parents were proud, and now he is very excited about what the future holds.

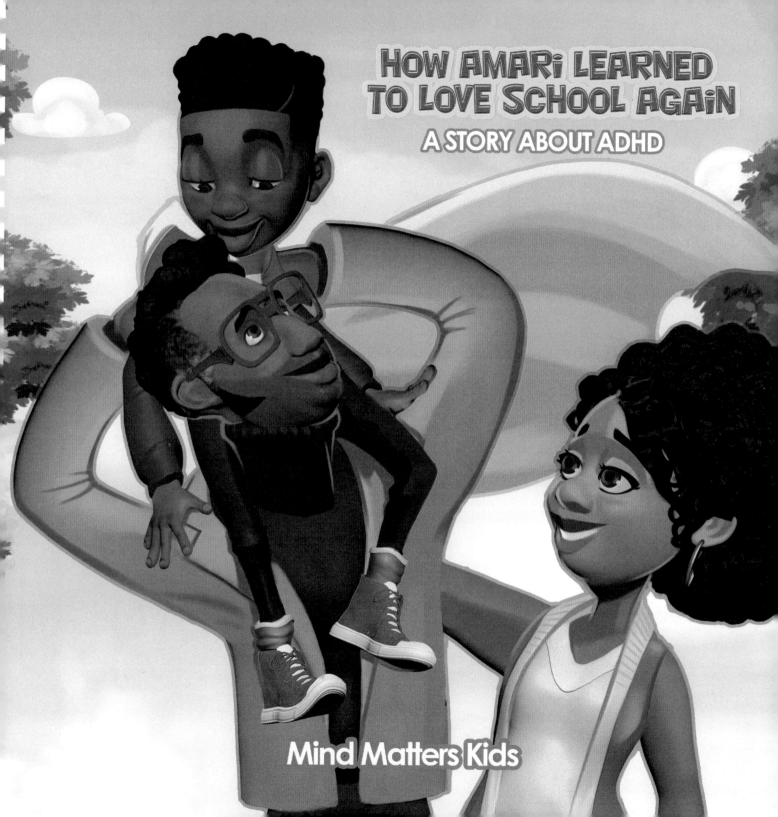

About the Authors:

Global Health Psychiatry, LLC is made up of 10 visionary black psychiatrists (Otis Anderson III, MD, Timothy G. Benson, MD, Malaika Berkeley, MD, MPH, Delane Casiano, MD, Ericka Goodwin, MD, Napoleon Higgins, Jr., MD, James Lee, Jr., MD, Michael Pratts, MD, Karriem Salaam, MD, Teo-Carlo Straun, MD) who share a passion for empowering the black community about mental health issues. They wrote this book to provide further education about ADHD in a way that is fun and child friendly to inform children and families with an added bonus of educational materials provided for adults. They have also written the book Mind Matters: A Resource Guide to Psychiatry for Black Communities. Both books focus on making mental health concepts easier to understand by translating them into common everyday language.

Please visit our website and follow us on social media.
http://www.GHPsychiatry.org
info@ghpsychiatry.com
Twitter and Instagram@GHPsychiatry
www.facebook.com/GHPsychiatry

The Illustrator:

Tyrus Goshay is an award-winning digital illustrator and 3D artist with over 18 years of experience. He serves as a college professor, teaching both game design, and illustration in his off time. Tyrus has a bachelor's in Computer Animation and Multimedia and a master's degree in Teaching With Technology (MALT). He has contributed to several award-winning projects in the world of toy design and has been recognized for his achievements in academia as well. He also has tutorials in illustration and digital sculpting available on the web.

Visit his bookstore, and see other books that he has illustrated.

www.tgosketch.bigcartel.com
Facebook.Com/tgosketch
tgosketch@gmail.com
Instagram/tgosketch

Mind Matters Kids

1. What are Amari's challenges in school?
2. Before going to see the doctor, how did Amari feel about school?
- After seeing the doctor?
3. Before going to see the doctor, how did Amari feel about himself?
- After seeing the doctor?

PARENT INFORMATION:

WHAT DOES ADHD STAND FOR?

ADHD stands for Attention Deficit Hyperactivity Disorder. ADHD is one of the most common reasons that Children are assessed for mental health treatment. Sometimes people also commonly refer to this as ADD which is an older, slightly different term.

WHAT IS THE DIFFERENCE BETWEEN ADD AND ADHD?

ADD (Attention Deficit Disorder) was renamed ADHD, so both refer to the same mental health issue, but ADHD is the current official clinical name. There are subtypes to describe whether there is significant hyperactivity present, instead of it being represented by whether there is an "H" for hyperactivity in the name.

ARE THERE DIFFERENT TYPES OF ADHD?

ADHD is broken down into multiple subtypes: inattentive, hyperactive-impulsive, and combined presentation.

MY CHILD IS HYPERACTIVE AND DOES NOT PAY ATTENTION. DOES HE/SHE HAVE ADHD?

It is important to remember that inattention and hyperactivity are symptoms, not a diagnosis. These symptoms can occur in a variety of conditions or at times of stress in a child's life, which is why it is important to have your child evaluated by a professional to determine the cause of these symptoms.

WHEN ARE ADHD SYMPTOMS USUALLY FIRST OBSERVED?

ADHD symptoms are usually first noticed when a child starts school, day care, or when the child is around other children and another adult notices that the child's behavior is significantly different from other children of a similar age. By comparison, children with ADHD will be far more inattentive, hyperactive, or both. Teachers and day care workers will point this out to parents, which should prompt a visit to a pediatrician, child psychiatrist, or psychologist. There are currently no blood tests, brain scans, or genetic tests for ADHD.

WHAT ARE THE SYMPTOMS OF ADHD?

The symptoms of ADHD fall into two main categories: inattention and hyperactive-impulsive.

Examples of inattention include:
- Inability to pay attention to details.
- Difficulty sustaining attention
- Difficulty completing tasks such as chores or schoolwork
- Difficulty organizing
- Difficulty listening
- Avoiding or disliking doing things that require sustained attention
- Losing things frequently
- Getting distracted easily
- Forgetting things

EXAMPLES OF HYPERACTIVE-IMPULSIVE INCLUDE:

- Fidgeting with hands or feet
- Squirming in a chair
- Frequently getting up when staying seated is expected
- Running or climbing excessively
- Acting on the go or constantly moving
- Talking excessively
- Blurting out answers before questions are completed
- Having trouble waiting or taking turns
- Interrupting or intruding on what others are saying or doing

Adapted from Diagnostic and Statistical Manual of Mental Disorders (5th ed.) Or DSM-5

WHAT HAPPENS DURING AN EVALUATION FOR ADHD?

Initial evaluations usually consist of a review of the child's medical history, diet, medications, and major changes in the child's life. It is helpful to bring report cards and any documentation from teachers or others who are around the child in an organized setting to help further aid in the evaluation. In addition, parents and teachers are often asked to complete rating scales for assessing ADHD.

WHY IS IT IMPORTANT TO TREAT ADHD?

There are social, emotional, and educational benefits for treating ADHD. Early treatment could help children with ADHD learn to control their behavior in and out of school. Behavioral control is important for children's social interactions with other children and adults. Untreated ADHD could lead to behavioral challenges and social isolation that could negatively affect a child's self-esteem, such as feeling depressed from struggling at school or at home.

Children with untreated ADHD could also be excluded from educational and extracurricular opportunities, resulting in limited options for their future. It is important for parents/caregivers to know that ADHD is a very treatable condition. Delaying or avoiding ADHD treatment could leave children to suffer unnecessarily.

WHY IS IT IMPORTANT TO TREAT ADHD?

There are social, emotional, and educational benefits for treating ADHD. Early treatment could help children with ADHD learn to control their behavior in and out of school. Behavioral control is important for children's social interactions with other children and adults. Untreated ADHD could lead to behavioral challenges and social isolation that could negatively affect a child's self-esteem, such as feeling depressed from struggling at school or at home. Children with untreated ADHD could also be excluded from educational and extracurricular opportunities, resulting in limited options for their future. It is important for parents/caregivers to know that ADHD is a very treatable condition. Delaying or avoiding ADHD treatment could leave children to suffer unnecessarily.

DID I DO SOMETHING TO CAUSE MY CHILD'S ADHD?

There is no single known cause of ADHD. It is a medical condition that results from a chemical imbalance in the brain.

WHAT ARE THE TREATMENTS FOR ADHD?

You should know that there is no cure for ADHD; however, there are many effective treatment options that include behavior therapy, medications, and school accommodations.

WHAT IS BEHAVIOR THERAPY FOR ADHD?

The goals of behavior therapy are to learn or strengthen positive behaviors and eliminate unwanted or problematic behaviors. Behavior therapy includes training for parents, working with the children, or a combination of the two. Teachers also use behavior therapy to help reduce problem behaviors at school.

WHAT ARE THE MEDICATION OPTIONS FOR ADHD?

Medication options for ADHD could be divided into two broad categories: stimulants and nonstimulants. The most common types of medication used for treating ADHD are called stimulants. The unique thing about stimulants is that they work right away and don't need to build up in the person's system before they are effective. Some common stimulant medications are methylphenidate (Concerta, Metadate, Ritalin), dextroamphetamine/amphetamine (Adderall), dextroamphetamine (Dexedrine), lisdexamfetamine (Vyvanse).

Unlike stimulant medications that work immediately, nonstimulant medications may take days to weeks to work. The most common nonstimulant medications are atomoxetine (Strattera), bupropion (Wellbutrin), guanfacine (Tenex, Intuniv), and clonidine (Catapres, Kapvay).

Please refer to Mind Matters: A Resource Guide to Psychiatry for Black Communities (2018) for more detailed information about medications.

IS MEDICATION SAFE?

Many people worry that medication will change their personality or make them seem like a "zombie." The goal of medication is to help the child function at their best, not to seem like someone else. Also, appearing "zombie-like" is not a common side effect.

Some fear that medications will be addictive, especially the stimulants. It is important to be aware that stimulants are controlled substances due to their abuse potential. However, appropriately treated individuals with ADHD have a lower risk of future addictive behavior. As with any medication, there can be side effects. Medication treatment must be closely monitored. If there are any problems, the medication needs to be reassessed.

HOW LONG DOES MY CHILD NEED TO TAKE THE MEDICATION?

It is recommended to take the medication until symptoms are no longer present and medications are no longer needed to manage symptoms. For many individuals, the symptoms will persist, but for some, the symptoms may resolve with time.

HOW DO SCHOOLS ACCOMMODATE ADHD BEHAVIOR?

- There are a variety of school-based interventions for ADHD. Some examples include:
- Seating the child in the front of the class
- Making direct eye contact and approaching the child when speaking to them
- Going over a list of the child's assignments and sending it home with the child
- Giving single-step instructions
- Breaking tasks into smaller chunks
- Providing frequent, positive feedback
- Integrating movement breaks throughout the day
- Keeping the child near the teacher or teacher's aid during transitions

These can be done formally or informally. Formal plans may include a 504 plan or an Individualized Educational Plan (IEP). These will be discussed further. ADHD is not related to intelligence and does not mean that a child cannot learn.

WHY IS MY CHILD BEING PLACED IN SPECIAL EDUCATION?

School funding for accommodations frequently falls under the umbrella of "Special Education." It does not mean that your child is "slow" or unable to learn. In fact, many gifted programs are also part of Special Education.

WHAT IS THE DIFFERENCE BETWEEN AN IEP AND 504?

Both of these are formal plans that include school accommodations for students that can help with behavioral, emotional, and learning issues. IEPs are more specific than 504 plans, while 504 plans can be applied more broadly. Both of these plans should be requested in writing, and the school should complete formal testing prior to developing either type of plan.

IN SCHOOL, HOW CAN I ADVOCATE FOR MY CHILD DIAGNOSED WITH ADHD?

There are many ways for parents/caregivers of children with ADHD to advocate for their children.
* The child should be evaluated by a pediatrician, primary care provider, psychiatrist or other mental health professional to confirm the diagnosis of ADHD.
* The evaluation, including treatment recommendations, should be used by the child's school to create and implement a plan to meet the student's educational needs.
* Parents should confirm that their child's school is able to provide the services and support necessary to educate their child with ADHD. The parent should request an Individualized Education Plan (IEP) or a 504 plan in writing. Most schools are equipped and willing to provide services. If they are unwilling, there are educational lawyers that can help if you need further assistance.
* The parent should make sure the IEP or 504 is updated every year.
* The parent should communicate regularly and work together with the child's teacher(s) to develop learning strategies for the home and classroom.
* The parent should also insist that the child be fully evaluated for strengths and skills.

IS ADHD DIAGNOSED MORE FREQUENTLY IN SOME CULTURES/RACES?

It is believed that more children and adolescents in the African American community are diagnosed with ADHD. However, due to racism and bias, African American children are less likely to be accurately diagnosed with ADHD and more likely to be incorrectly diagnosed with more severe behavioral disorders such as Conduct Disorder or Oppositional Defiant Disorder. Many African American children are often labeled as being "bad" when they are actually exhibiting symptoms of a mental health condition which is causing challenging behaviors.

WHAT ARE OTHER ISSUES THAT CAN CAUSE SYMPTOMS SIMILAR TO ADHD?

Family conflict, trauma, poor nutrition, sleep deprivation, fetal alcohol exposure, maternal substance use (Including smoking), environmental toxins, and undiagnosed learning disorders/disabilities can all present with some of the same symptoms as ADHD. In addition, problems coping with stress can present in a similar fashion.

DO CHILDREN GROW OUT OF ADHD?

About one-third of children will have symptoms that resolve as an adult. More often, the hyperactivity behavior will decrease as the child matures, but the inattention behavior is less likely to go away.

WHAT ELSE CAN I, AS A PARENT, DO TO HELP?

It is important to have patience with your child and to reinforce how much you love them. Children can internalize what adults say, so it is important to avoid language that labels the child as "bad." You also need to get help as soon as you suspect there is a problem, and you should continue to advocate for your child's needs in the community, at school, and with healthcare providers.

For more information on this subject or other mental health topics, please refer to Mind Matters: A Resource Guide to Psychiatry for Black Communities or visit

www.GHPsychiatry.org

Otis Anderson, III, MD, Timothy G. Benson, MD, Malaika Berkeley, MD, Delane Casiano, MD, Ericka Goodwin,MD, Napoleon B. Higgins, Jr., MD, James Lee, Jr., MD, Michael Pratts, MD, Karriem Salaam, MD, and Teo-Carlo Straun, MD. Mind Matters: A Resource Guide to Psychiatry for Black Communities. North Charleston, SC: KDP Independent Publishing Platform, 2018.

American Psychiatric Association. Diagnostic and Statistical Manual of Mental Disorders. 5th ed. Washington, DC: American Psychiatric Association, 2013.

Mind Matters Kids

Made in the USA
Columbia, SC
28 June 2019